Haunted Lovers: Ghosts of Castillo de San Marcos

M. Jordan

DEDICATION

To Clint, Lacey, and Caelan.

CONTENTS

ACKNOWLEDGMENTS

I would like to extend my appreciation to the U.S. Department of Interior's National Park Service and the City of St. Augustine for their dedication to the preservation and maintenance of our historic National Monument, Castillo de San Marcos.

CHAPTER ONE

BACKGROUND

I am neither a ghost hunter, paranormal investigator, nor self-proclaimed expert in anything unseen. In fact, I am not even a writer. Therefore, I request the reader's tolerance in advance for this most unrefined narrative. In addition, please know that mere words seem insufficient to fully describe my experience. Nevertheless, I will do my best to tell you what happened. Whether you believe it or not is entirely up to you.

I want you to know that this is not my story. This story belongs to the haunted lovers of the Castillo De San Marcos in St. Augustine, Florida who want you, the reader, to know "what happened".

The Photographs

Photographs relating to this paranormal experience in the Castillo's Powder Room were taken on February 10, 2013 with an IPhone 4. While the photos are excellent, in no way do they reveal everything I was able to see with my eyes when the camera flashed. Much of what was visible in the room during the flash was not big or bright enough to be picked up by the IPhone camera.

During the encounter I attempted to capture moving images with the video component of my IPhone because I thought it would provide more compelling evidence of something paranormal. Unfortunately, very low light inside the room proved to be insufficient for this purpose.

CHAPTER TWO

UNSOLICITED ENCOUNTER

According to paranormal researchers, ghost hunters, and numerous visitors of St. Augustine, Florida, there are a number of legendary spirits roaming around town. Because St. Augustine is the oldest city in America, there is a lot of interesting history to discover. Some people visit St. Augustine for its beauty, others for its history, and others for its ghosts.

A very popular website or tourists and locals known s *Ghost Report* contains information on all things haunted in St. Augustine. It has good information for anyone who may be searching for actively paranormal locations. In addition, Ghost Report specifically addresses paranormal activity in the historic National Monument known as Castillo de San Marcos, the focus of this book. Ghost Report(www.ghostreport.com/states/florida/CastilloDeSanMarc

os.htm) states, "A number of employees and guests take pictures around the fort to discover orbs, rods, and strange mists in them. Ghost videos have been made that show what appear to be tiny lights moving around the structure and even blurs passing in front of the video camera."

As I mentioned previously, this is good information for those seeking some type of paranormal experience, but I am *not* one of those people. In fact, I take care *not* to pursue anything that would be considered paranormal. Having said that, sometimes things happen without outside our scope of control; they are completely unsolicited. This is what happened to me on February 10, 2013, while visiting the Castillo de San Marcos in St. Augustine, Florida.

Clint and I happen to be residents of Florida. It is often fun to take short trips around the State playing "tourists". We view this as a major perk for living in the great Sunshine State. On this particular day, Clint and I planned to spend our time visiting the city of St. Augustine, Florida. With so many interesting things to do and see in St. Augustine, it seemed wise for us to get an early start.

The primary purpose of our trip, and source of my excitement, was the opportunity to visit the old fort. We had driven by this landmark many times and admired the way its massive architecture dominates the west shore of the St. Johns River. Consequently the historic Castillo de San Marcos was our first destination for the day.

Previously, I heard mention of guests and locals seeing ghosts and other apparitions in St. Augustine and more specifically in and around the old fort. However, we were not looking for ghosts. Quite to the contrary. We were simply interested in the fort for its historical significance and architectural design.

It was a bright and virtually cloudless morning; the temperature was cool with very little humidity. The day seemed perfect for taking photographs and walking around. Since I knew almost nothing about the fort other than its obvious purpose and landmark status, I began my visit with no specific expectations.

Clint and I arrived at Castillo De San Marcos around 8:45 a.m. Since it was early, we were among the first few visitors to enter the fort. Like all National Monuments, we knew this would be a wonderful learning experience for both of us.

Upon our approach, a Park Service employee dressed in clothing of the period, stood at the end of the sidewalk greeting visitors. As we approached him, he asked, "Do you know why this is called a Castillo, or castle, instead of a fort?" We did not know, so he explained, "It's because there is a drawbridge." He further explained that the drawbridge was necessary because of the moat." I made a mental note to recall this important distinction for any future conversations pertaining to my visit.

Next, we advanced to the admissions hut where we purchased our tickets and received a map along with other information. We then entered the Castillo via the walkway and drawbridge, pausing for a couple of photographs along the way.

The following photographs are the first pictures taken before we entered the walls of the Castillo.

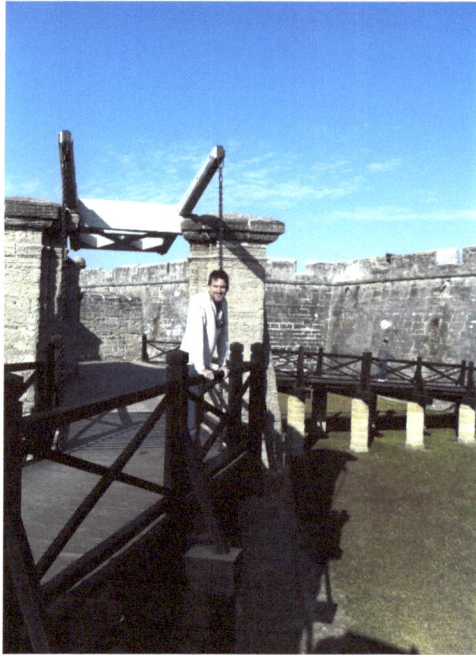

Photo 1: Clint on the drawbridge

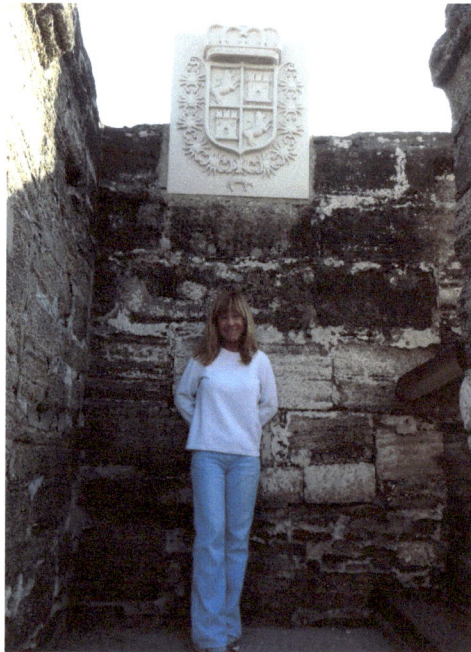

Photo 2: Me in front of the Two Lions crest.

Whenever we are in a "tourist" mode, regardless of the location, Clint and I behave very differently. Clint enjoys walking around at a calculated pace then reading every sign and informational marker. He likes to stand there awhile thinking about what he just read. After that, he likes to spend even more time taking pictures from various creative angles. Doing all of this takes a lot of time.

In contrast, I like to read only the headlines of signs. I then skim the text for main ideas, but generally I do not bother with the details. In fact, I might skip over the text altogether depending whether or not I am in a hurry. If I really want to know more then I read the signs thoroughly. This strategy works best for me, because I believe it gives me an opportunity to both see and "feel" the setting. I like to get the big picture first then review the details later. Unfortunately, as a result of my own behavior, I occasionally find that I have overlooked important information describing the site. This is especially apparent when talking to Clint about something we have seen or some place we have been. He tends to remember the details.

Because of our different strategies for looking

around, this day was no different. Clint and I were usually not in close proximity to one another. In fact, throughout much of our visit, we were in different parts of the Castillo altogether. I progressed through the first few rooms of the Castillo much more rapidly than Clint.

While in between the various rooms I occasionally paused to enjoy the sunshine in the courtyard. Clint was still reading signs somewhere so I took a more photos of the old doorways. I was particularly interested in one room where supplies such as old barrels, lanterns, and other items had been stored and were on display. I stood outside looking through window for a long time reflecting on all the history of that room. It felt like something or someone invisible might be there so I kept looking. Since I didn't see anything unusual I dismissed my feelings and moved on.

Photo 3: Courtyard doorway

Knowing that Clint was still about ten minutes behind my me, I proceeded on around the courtyard from west to east. I made my way into a large room in the northeast corner of the Castillo. I don't remember the purpose of room nor do I even remember looking at the sign describing its purpose. I only recall feeling cautiously concerned about the connecting room.

There was no one around so I just listened quietly to the thoughts and feelings in my head. Something seemed a little "odd" about the doorway but sensing nothing specific I approached the room slowly, peered through the doorway, then seeing no one, I walked in. I only stepped into the room approximately a foot or two. I simply could not move forward because I had an overwhelming sense of a presence there in the room with me.

The thick coquina stone walls absorb all sound so the room was extremely quiet. Having no windows or openings other than the interior doorway, the room was really dark. It was also very narrow and deep with a high arched ceiling. I opened my eyes as wide as possible to see if there was something in the room with me. I could not confirm with my eyes what I was feeling so I continued to stand silently trying to analyze what I was sensing.

Within approximately 10 seconds I felt something move "into" the full length of only the left side of my body. It felt like someone was leaning into me or hovering over me but only just on my left side. Whatever it was, it felt much larger than me and it was absolutely ice cold, but it was coldest on my left side. Accompanying this presence was an icy swirling breeze. It felt like a light weight scarf was blowing around my neck. As this breeze blew around my neck I could hear a faint "whooshing" noise near my ears. Not only did I feel as though I was about to be frozen in place, my entire body also felt like it had a low-voltage charge flowing through it. All of my skin felt like it was "buzzing".

Even through my long sleeve shirt, I could feel every

hair on my arms standing straight up. Goose bumps completely covered me. Thinking this was bizarre, I pulled my sleeves up to look at the goose bumps and hair on my arms. All the while, my teeth were chattering from the frigid temperature encompassing my body. Although this was completely startling both physically and emotionally, I knew immediately what was happening - something or someone not made of flesh and blood was standing over me. I was not consumed with fear, but I was still too afraid to move.

I don't really know exactly why I didn't scream in horror and run out of the room. The best explanation I can offer is that I did not sense that the presence to be evil or demonic. My physical reaction was most concerning since I would never expect something like this to happen at 9:15 in the morning. Even so, I was inclined to stand my ground until I could more logically determine why this was happening and what, if anything, I should do about it.

While it felt like a long time, it was probably only a matter of seconds before I was able to assemble some logical thoughts. I decided to accept the fact that this was happening and deal with it until I could get a better idea of who or what it was.

Since I had been taking photos in the courtyard, my

IPhone was still in my right hand. I raised the IPhone, aimed it toward the front of the room, and began taking photos. Because I was holding the cell phone higher than my line of vision, I could not see what was in the photos.

In retrospect, admit that I simply did not have the courage to aim the camera toward my left shoulder. I really didn't want to see what was standing over me. Still, I gathered enough courage to lower the IPhone so I could look at the images in the camera. I thought if anything else was there maybe I would be able to see it.

Now, with my IPhone pointed toward the front of the room, I began taking pictures. I could clearly see that I was not alone. I felt both alarmed and amazed. In the light of my camera there were orbs of various sizes flying all around the room in what seemed to be purposeful yet erratic directions similar to what bats do when they are catching mosquitos. Some of the orbs were bright and wide while others were small and delicate. I was more fascinated than afraid because I had never seen anything like it. I was especially shocked by *quantity* of things flying around that I couldn't see with my naked eyes.

I could see and feel orbs flying around me because they would zoom over the top of my head as they headed toward the front of the room. Some of them made a couple of laps from the front to the back then disappear into the coquina walls. This too was weird. At first when they "hit" the wall I thought they might squish or blow up. Instead, they easily went in and out of the walls without resistance. A few seconds later I would see an orb pop out of the same wall and zoom around. Once I realized what was happening I became completely engrossed in observing all the activity.

I heard Clint enter the room next to me so I yelled, "Clinton, come here! Hurry! There's ghost in this room! He is standing right next to me. Hurry up!" Clint replied, "Stop yelling; you're going to create a scene or something." I said, "Okay, but hurry!"

Clint walked through the doorway and stood next to me. He was unable step into the room very far because I was still standing firm in my original spot. With my teeth still chattering from the cold I said, "Look at me. I'm freezing! Look at the hair on my arms. Do you see it? Look at these giant goose bumps. Something is in here, Clint. I'm telling you – I can see them on my cell phone!" He said, "Okay. Calm down. I don't see anything." I replied, "Sorry, but I can see all kinds of things flying through the room when I snap photos with my cell phone!"

Clint is very calm. While he could see the hair on my arms standing up as well as the goose bumps, he told me that he could not see or feel a ghost standing over me. In fact, when Clint walked up to me and stood at the left side of my body, the coldness slowly lifted off of me. This was a relief because the extremely cold temperature was most unpleasant.

Since Clint was unable to see or feel anything unusual he didn't seem to be alarmed. Then predictably, Clint walked up to the sign to read the information about the room. While he did this I kept taking photos.

I said, "Clinton, there are orbs flying right over the top of you and around you. Can't you see them?" He said, "I don't see anything." I said, "Well, I am standing here taking pictures of them flying right over you."

Upon reading the sign, Clint informed me that we were standing in the Powder Room where many animals and other bones were buried. He said the room had been sealed for a hundred years. He also informed me that there were local myths of lovers who died in the room. After standing there a few minutes more, Clint decided to move on with his tour. I, on the other hand, remained in the room.

I walked a bit further into the room remaining close to

the doorway probably no more than 2 feet from where I originally felt the cold presence of the ghost. I was definitely not keen on wandering too far from the only exit. This wasn't really fear; I was just being "respectfully cautious". I also believed that moving around might create a disruption to whatever was happening, which, in turn, might limit my experience, and understanding.

Whenever the camera flashed I observed that orbs were different sizes. Each one was translucent and glowing. In addition, each orb had a thin glowing external ring. Most of the orbs appeared a bluish white, light yellow, or light neon green. As they flew around they left light trails behind them. I was struck by the fact that there were so many of them going in different directions. I noticed that they were able to fly very fast like a hummingbird. I also noticed they were able to accelerate, decelerate, and immediately change in direction without adjusting their speed. Furthermore, the orbs were neither in anyway neither limited by thick coquina walls nor detoured in any way by the presence of human beings. Since I had no way of knowing *why* they were moving around as they were I could only speculate .

Because the orbs were still passing through the walls I

went back into the other room to see if they were coming out of the wall on the other side. I took a couple of pictures in the other room where I thought they would exit if they were traveling in a straight line, but I didn't see anything. (Since that room was sunny it might have been too bright to see them with my camera.)

Now that I was feeling confident that I could observe the activity critically I went back into the Powder Room. If I should have been afraid I wasn't. In fact, the longer I stood taking pictures more relaxed I became. For whatever reason, the whooshing breezes and erratic movements from all of these orbs became more and more humorous. I remember thinking the orbs were silly in their appearance and behavior.

Watching the orbs zoom around reminded me of a toy poodle I had as a child. When the poodle would become really happy and excited she would suddenly start running extremely fast in circles through the house. With her ears back and a crazy look in her eyes she would run and run. My family and I would all just laugh as we watched the dog tear past. We could hear her toenails digging into the carpet like a screeching car on a tight turn. Likewise, I imagined the orbs were "excited" about something. I even wondered if they were spirits of deceased cats and dogs playing around.

Next, having come to the conclusion that these paranormal entities did not seem malicious, I walked up to the sign so I could see what it said. I aimed my IPhone over the top of the sign took more pictures. (I needed to take more pictures because it was the only way I could see what was happening.) In the camera's flash I could see several orbs moving slowly both horizontally and diagonally through the space between the wall, the sign, and myself. Upon noticing a far higher concentration of tiny orbs, I pointed my IPhone toward the ground and began taking yet more pictures. I could see the tiny orbs when I snapped the pictures but they were not bright enough to generate an image in the actual photographs (or so I thought). Nevertheless, I continued taking pictures because there appeared to be more and more tiny orbs coming out of the ground.

Even though my own natural eyesight and my ability to take photographs quickly was a limitation, I could tell something different was definitely happening. I began seeing thousands of tiny orbs. These tiny orbs were forming a thick blanket of glowing "pinpoints" that slowly rose up out of the dirt floor then just hovered. This sight was so unusual in comparison to all the other strange things taking place in the room I thought it must be especially important.

I tried to debunk what I was seeing as dust particles, then I realized this type of movement would be inconsistent with the movement of dust particles. In addition, the tiny orbs were only rising from only certain parts of the ground rather than all of it, which didn't seem logical. Upon this realization I began to panic. I wondered if something horrifying was going to come out of the ground then grab me like something in the movies. I also thought now might be a good time to leave, but I was unsure if I should really turn my back since I didn't know what it was. In short, I was a rather "freaked out". On the other hand, it was so mesmerizing I couldn't leave. I didn't want to miss seeing whatever this was so I made the decision to keep looking.

I took a step to my right so I could stand closer to the wall. There I could see the ground clearly without looking over the top of the sign. I thought that if focused my attention more while taking pictures maybe I would have enough information to discern what was happening. I took a few more pictures then it really began to sink into my head that something significant was happening. Consequently, I stopped taking pictures and stood silently holding my IPhone to my side. I just stood there reflecting on my encounter. While it was all so interesting and a lot of fun to observe, this experience left me feeling very small and completely insignificant; it was profoundly humbling.

I wondered who these spirits were. Why were they presenting themselves in such a way that I could hear, see, and feel them? I thought more about the information on the sign telling of the many bones that had been buried in the room and the legend of the two lovers who died there. As I stood thinking, I became totally overwhelmed with a deep sense of sadness accompanied by intense love. I clearly recall thinking to myself, "I am so sorry. I am so very sorry for whatever happened to you."

Standing there with slightly teary eyes, I heard a soft, sustained, and whisper-like male voice say, "T-e-l-l t-h-e-m." This voice really startled me. Whoever or whatever this was now had my full attention. In response, I thought, "Tell them *what*?" I stood silent again thinking, "Tell them *what*?". Within just a few seconds, the same male voice whispered, "w-h-a-t h-a-p-p-e-n-e-d."

Upon hearing these words I thought, "What do you mean tell them what happened." "Who is *them*?" "How can I tell *them* when *I* don't even know what happened?"

At that point I didn't really know what to do. I was in

conflict because it seemed as though I could have stayed in the Powder Room taking photos all day. On the other hand there was so much more of the old fort to see and I was still feeling excited but confused.

It seemed best to locate Clint so I could get back into reality with the living and breathing. I did not take time to view the photographs on my phone even though I was certain some images had been captured. After all, I knew there would plenty of time to examine all the photos later on.

I located Clint, but he was still reading signs and taking pictures. I told him to take his time then we could go upstairs to look around and watch the cannons fire (a Sunday event at the Castillo). I walked to the bottom of the stairs to wait.

While waiting I began looking at my photos. I noticed that I had captured a number of orbs so I was quite thrilled. I asked one of the Park Service employees, who was also standing there, if she had ever seen any ghosts in the Castillo. She said that she was fairly new, although she worked nights on occasion. She indicated that she had seen couple of rats running around in the dark, but never a ghost. I pointed to the northeast corner of the courtyard and said, "Well, there's ghost in the Power Room right now. I just took a picture of it." I showed her all the orbs in one of my photos and said, "Something is going on in that room." She looked at the photo then she looked at me. She did not comment.

By about that time, Clint was finished so we walked upstairs. We both took some more pictures and we watched the cannon firing ritual. We sat there in the sun enjoying the beauty of the day and the overall setting of the old fort.

While sitting there with Clint I looked at my photographs then I showed them to him. He said the pictures were interesting and that I should take a closer look when I got home. Unsure about what he was thinking about all of this I decided not to offer any additional details regarding my experience. I didn't want to overwhelm him information that seemed unbelievable even to me.

In light of what was on my camera I suggested to Clint that we both return to the Powder Room. I wanted Clint to take photos with *his* IPhone this time so he could see for himself that something or someone was in the room. He agreed. Of course by this time of the morning there were many more visitors. I wondered if either of us would be able to see or feel anything when we returned.

As soon as I entered the Powder Room for the second time I began taking more pictures with my IPhone. I was relieved that a few orbs were still whooshing around because this seemed to be the perfect (and safe) opportunity for Clint to see something paranormal for himself. Unfortunately, he was unable to see anything with his naked eyes. He stood momentarily next to the left wall. Then he stepped to the front of the room and aimed his IPhone forward.

I asked if he could see anything, but he replied, "Nothing." I said, "Well, I don't understand it. I don't know what to tell you except that I can see them flying all around you and over the top of your head. I just took another picture of them."

Just then, some other people walked into the room to look around. While I continued taking pictures I could see the orbs above some woman as she walked through the room, but I did not think it appropriate to bring this to her attention. In fact, I waited until they all left to say any more about the orbs to Clint. I didn't want to embarrass him or frighten the other visitors.

Clint decided to walk outside and look around some more. As before, I told him I wanted to take a few more pictures then I would join him, which is what I did. We walked around awhile longer then left to find a nice restaurant where we could have lunch.

During lunch I began flipping through the photos, but I really wanted to stay present in the moment with Clint so I put the IPhone away. We both realized there were some great pictures of something paranormal but we agreed would look at them together later in the evening when we got home.

That evening, Clint and I took time to sit and study the photographs. Then, I was able to see things I had not been able to see even when taking the pictures. The significance of these pictures began to become apparent. I then realized that the ghostly images in my photographs were much more than a legend - they were the lovers who died tragically in the Powder Room.

As I began to contemplate the mixture of my paranormal experience with factual information on the sign, pieces of this peculiar mystery began to come together. Even though I could not (and *still* do not) fully comprehend what happened, it seemed this was not some obscure or random paranormal experience. These spirits had a deeply personal story *and* they wanted someone to tell it on their behalf.

Photo 1: Powder Room. This was the first photo. Note the male face on the upper rear of the right wall.

Photo 2: Mist and orbs in the Power Room. Faces of a man and woman are visible on the bricks of the rear and right wall. It is unclear whether these are natural arrangements of the stone or something more. The female face shows delicate facial features.

Photo 3: Multiple orbs and mist with a large center orb.
A light trail is visible on the left side of the photo.

Photo 8: Clint reading the sign. Orbs over his head, in front of him, to the right side of the sign, and more mist.

Photo 10: Orb "examining" Clint's IPhone. Another orb under the sign and on right wall. Greenish bar on Clint's left arm inconsistent with other shadows.

Photo 11: Clint with faces in the brick immediately to the right of his face (back and right walls). Mist on right wall.

Photo 15: Orbs low to the ground behind the sign.

Photo 16: White mist above the shadow cast by the sign. The mist is clearly above the shadow.

Photo 17: White mist shows lovers embracing face to face.

Photo 18: Haunted lovers and orbs above them.

Photo 19: Lovers' mist and orb at top of center wall.

Photo 20: White orb flying above the mist.

Photo 21:   Haunted lovers, other mist, and orb light trail.

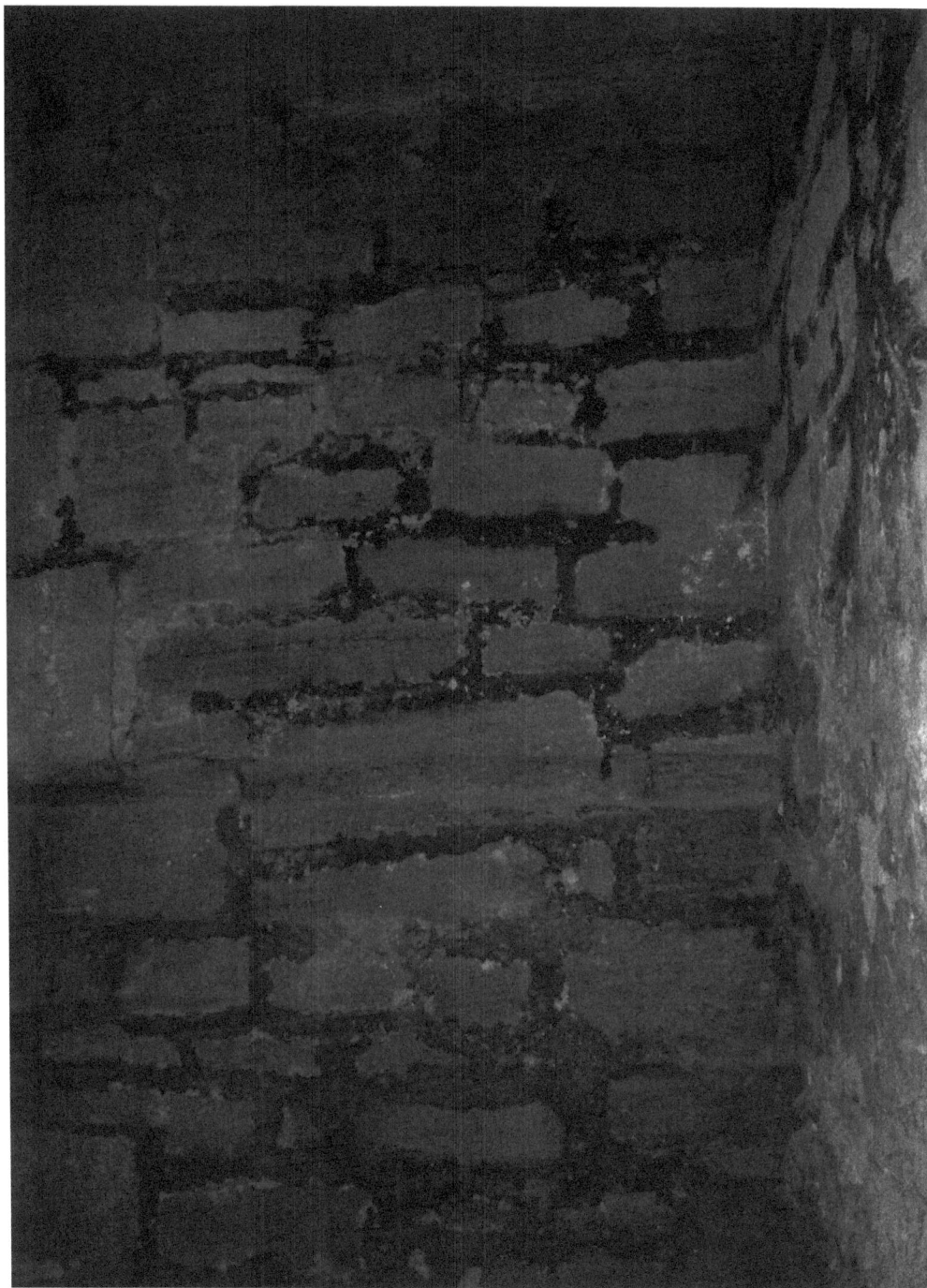

Photo 23: Mist and faces in the bricks. Female center wall, male right wall at same height.

Photo 24: Mist and more orbs.

Photo 36: Clint surrounded by orbs with light trails.
Another visitor's arm is visible in the lower right corner.

CHAPTER THREE

THE SETTING

The Castillo de San Marcos is the most important relic of Florida's Spanish heritage. It is the oldest fort in the United States. According to Harrington, Manucy, & Goggin, 1956, archeological excavations revealed that when the Spaniards landed at the Tumucua Indian village in 1565, they "immediately set to work throwing up earthworks around the aboriginal structure". For nearly 100 years, and for various reasons, the fort withstood multiple cycles of destruction followed by re-construction.

In 1672 the Spanish built the "permanent fort of stone, called Castillo de San Marcos". Then between 1738-1739 the Castillo was enlarged and modernized to accommodate military demands. The modernization included major changes that included removal of an L-shaped structure in the center of the courtyard and replacement of the rooms around the perimeter of the courtyard. These courtyard rooms "were replaced with the large, massively-arched rooms standing today." In fact, a 1675 sketch of the Castillo courtyard indicates placement of the arch for powder in the same location as currently labeled by the U.S. Interior Department's National Park Service. Thus, anyone visiting the Castillo today can easily appreciate all that is involved in preserving this historic relic.

More specific information about the Castillo's history from the time it was built in 1672 through the 1900's can be found from many different sources. One of the more descriptive timelines offering a basic overview of the Castillo can be found on one of the "tourist" websites: www.staugustine.com/history/castillo-de-san-marcos. In addition, our National Park Services also has excellent resources that provide historic information from 1672 to our present day. The website for this information is: http://www.nps.gov/casa/historyculture/index.htm.

CHAPTER FOUR

GHOSTS IDENTIFIED

In 1784, Colonel Marti, a Spanish officer, was ordered to oversee military operations at the Castillo de San Marcos. As assigned, Colonel Marti and his wife Mari relocated to St. Augustine, Florida. Some time thereafter, Mari had an affair with one of the officers named Captain Manual Abela. Unfortunately, the Colonel discovered that his wife and his officer were having an affair (or so it is alleged). Then, in a jealous rage, Colonel Marti had Mari and Manual chained to the dungeon walls where they were abandoned and left to die.

There are alternate and biased versions of this story, no doubt embellished by their authors over many decades. These embellishments may have contributed to the notion that the tale is mere legend. For example, in one version of the story, Mari Marti was said to have had a "roving eye" for all the men in the fort. She supposedly lured Captain Abela with her charm until he was completely ensnared. Once discovered by a soldier loyal to his Colonel, the soldier informed the poor Colonel of his unfaithful wife's transgression.

In yet another version of the story, Colonel Marti was said to be much older than Mari. Because the Colonel was consumed with his military career, he had no time for his beautiful young wife. Lonely and far from her family ties in Spain, Mari took comfort in the arms of Captain Abela.

Without specific historical details, the true nature of Mari and Manual's relationship will remain a mystery. Yet, one thing is absolutely certain - Colonel Marti was raging with jealousy. Consequently, the manifestation of negative behaviors relating to the Colonel's rage were predictable; "…for jealousy arouses a husband's fury, and he will show no mercy when he takes revenge" (Proverbs 6:34, NIV). Overflowing with such an intense burning jealousy, Colonel Marti swiftly ordered his wife Mari and Manual Abela to the dungeon where they were shackled to the wall.

There, in dark and impenetrable walls of the Castillo dungeon, Mari and Manual died. The couple suffered excruciating physical pain from dehydration and starvation.

They were further forced to endure the emotional torture of watching each other suffer. Yet, in spite of this horrific final chapter of their lives, Mari and Manual took comfort in each other's arms as they passed from life into eternity.

If the couple initially hoped for some merciful reprieve it never came. Since no one rescued the lovers, one might assume the Colonel issued an order against it. In fact, "for a long time, screams could be heard coming from the couple as they called for help. Eventually, the screams stopped" (www.ghostreport.com/states/florida/CastilloDeSanMarcos.htm).

It should be noted that according to *Bloomfield's Illustrated Historical Guide* of the late 19th century, "Under the northeast bastion we find a dark, gloomy dungeon twenty feet long, six feet wide, and nearly five feet high, where not a ray of light can penetrate. This was once built up, and cut off from all communication with the rest of the fort."

For over a hundred years there were individual reports of moans and crying coming from the dungeon area of the Castillo, but with no tangible indication of the source. Then, on the "21st day of July in the year 1833, a canon

actually cracked a floor. When this happened, the depths
of the fort were exposed. Upon investigation, the room in
which the lovers had been placed was exposed and the
skeletons were found, holding each other"
(www.hauntedflorida.com/haunted.htm).

The haunted lovers were not the only ones who died in
the Castillo, however. Later, in 1836, a former resident
of St. Augustine who was said to have witnessed the
terreplein of the northwest bastion falling in stated:

> "I stood upon the edge and looked down into this
> dungeon, and there saw the complete skeleton of a
> human being, lying at full length apparently on its
> back; the arms were extended from the body and the
> skeleton fingers were wide open; there appeared to be
> a gold ring upon one of the fingers. Encircling the
> wrists were iron bands, attached to which were chain
> fastened to a hasp in the coquina wall near the
> entrance to the dungeon" (Bloomfield, 1883, p.
> unknown).

Other historical accounts indicate there may have been some
form of strategic ignorance regarding of the deaths and
burials that occurred in the dungeon. Bloomfield (1883)
goes on to note that iron cages containing human bones were

recovered from the dungeon after 1836 then later secured by the Smithsonian Institute at Washington.

Conflicting accounts from "credible" sources regarding bones in the dungeon at the Castillo continued. The Florida Press quoted a lecture given by medical doctor J. Hume Simons. The quote reads:

> "The broken cage, with all the bones, except those which I hold in my hand, were buried in the sand mound to the north of the fort. I recognize these as portions of the tibia and fibula (or leg bones) of a female."

However, Joseph Henry of the Smithsonian provided the rebuttal to John L. Edwards, of Jacksonville, Florida in a letter where he states:

> "Sir: In reply to your letter of July 20th, we have to say that no objects such as those said to have been found in the dungeon of the old fort at St. Augustine have ever been received by us, although we are aware that the impression is otherwise."

A notation from Bloomfield (1883) states:

> "The finding of any bones is denied by Major W.H. Benham, U.S.A., on the authority of a Mr. Ridgely, Lieutenant Tuttle's overseer. Major Benham took charge

of the work upon the fort in January, 1839."

Since historic records are limited we are left to assemble what pieces we can to create a better picture of what happened. Given that less-than-flattering information often disappears from the record books, it is reasonable to conclude the legend of the lovers demise has real historic merit. Likewise there may also have been an attempt to conceal details of other deaths at the Castillo. At the very least, it is also possible that this type of recordkeeping was not viewed as important hundreds of years ago. We do know, however, the prisoners of the Castillo were shown no mercy. In fact, the military inflicted extremely cruel and gruesome punishments on prisoners for all types of crime. For example, prisoners were often suspended by chains or tortured by a rack "separating their joints and possibly tearing them literally apart" (www.ghosthearse.com/the-fortress-of-misery-st-augustine-florida).

CHAPTER FIVE

_____

UNDERSTANDING THE PARANORMAL

"Understanding the paranormal is like opening a book – once the book has been opened it can never be closed." Sheriff Doug of the Sheriff's Ghost Walk Tours, St. Augustine, FL

For thousands of years, people all around the world have claimed to have had paranormal encounters. This is nothing new. Yet, it is difficult to know where these people fall on the continuum of rational and intelligent all the way to delusional and cognitively challenged. No doubt, reports of the paranormal come from people on all points on the continuum. Unfortunately, there may be a disproportionate number of reports that seem less than credible. Because of this, it is important to question everything and try to debunk the stories from a scientific perspective whenever possible.

I am certainly no expert on spiritual matters or things relating to the paranormal. In fact I would be very skeptical of anyone who makes such a claim unless they provide compelling evidence to the contrary. Regardless, there *are* some general things to consider that might be helpful in a quest for a deeper understanding. To help expand our perspective I'm going offer just a few ideas along with some of my personal opinions.

Who Sees Ghosts?

If everyone saw ghosts there would be no controversy. Obviously, this is not the case. Not everyone has seen a ghost and not everyone will see a ghost. In fact, it is unlikely one's chance of having a paranormal experience would increase simply by wishing for it. Conversely, all attempts to avoid a paranormal experience are not likely to prevent it. So what is the difference between those who see ghosts and those who do not?

I tend to believe that all people share an equal possibility of having their own personal paranormal experience. On the other hand, paranormal experiences may only be the result of specific opportunities or being in the "right place at the right time". For this reason, I propose that equal possibilities do not necessarily result in equal opportunities. In my opinion, we are least likely to experience a random and unsolicited encounter. This doesn't mean we won't have one; it just means our chances are slim. In contrast, I believe that certain purposeful behaviors and activities may significantly increase our likelihood of having a paranormal experience.

Having said this, I am also of the opinion that some people may be predisposed (hard-wired) to experience the paranormal. These people may be more receptive or simply "available" to paranormal experiences. For whatever reason they are consciously and/or subconsciously "tuned in".

This touches on the "nature versus nurture" controversy, which is far too complex a discussion for this book. Still, we should at the very least ask, "Do we believe *because* we see, or do we see because we believe?" These questions are irrelevant to a skeptic or atheist, because they have no *reason* to believe. For the atheist, there is *absolutely* no God. Yet, claiming there is no God, is itself, an absolute. Thus, given there are no true absolutes, wouldn't the atheist at least say, "*What if* I am wrong?" Personally, I try to maintain a willingness to accept the possibility that my beliefs and opinions may be flawed. I believe we call this *learning*.

As for me, my unsolicited encounter with the haunted

lovers and other spirits in the Castillo was most likely a case of seeing *because* I believe. Whether nature or nurture, there are indications in my own history that contribute to my conclusion.

Generations of relatives (primarily on my father's side of the family) included morticians, fundamentalist Christians, and psychics. Often their philosophical beliefs were utterly incompatible, which led to some interesting debates. From my earliest recollection most family gatherings included storytelling about God, death, and the paranormal.

Orbs and Apparitions

Orbs and apparitions are strange and interesting. I really don't know much about them. Prior to my encounter, I had seen them in photographs and on television, but I am skeptical of this type of "evidence". I do know there is a growing interest in finding proof they exist. In addition, to those seeking information as a hobby, some spend a lot of time attempting serious research and trying to understand them. Regarding ghost orbs one author states:

> "Ghost orbs are able to move at very rapid speeds.
> They change directions at will, appear and disappear,
> and even seem to be hiding in some photographs. They

are curious by nature and actively seek out unsuspecting visitors. Ghost orbs are photographed almost everywhere there is a reported haunting. They have been photographed at the scenes of tragic accidents or at sites where tragedies occurred. Battlefields, cemeteries, and abandoned buildings are also very active sites for ghost orbs.

For the most part, ghost orbs simply want to attract attention. Perhaps they want to be noticed in order to covey a message to someone who is receptive to them. They may have some unfinished business that they are about. Remember, we cannot see them unless they want us to."
(http://www.llewellyn.com/journal/article/2037).

Apparently, it is one suggestion orbs need to conserve energy in case they need it for something "important". Therefore, they assume the shape of an orb because it requires less energy for something to manifest as an orb than a full-bodies ghost. Still, "at times they are able to appear denser or larger and they can manifest as a partial or full apparition"
(http://www.llewellyn.com/journal/article/2037).

Multiple Dimensions of Reality

For a number of years, physicists have been trying to prove whether or not multiple dimensions exist. They refer to multiple dimensions as superstrings and parallel worlds. If they *are* able to prove this then there will be absolute scientific proof we have been looking at reality through a very "flat" or one-dimensional perspective. This information would be difficult for some people to accept.

If you are not a believer in the paranormal, at least pretend for just a moment that multiple dimensions *do* exist. Locating them them might be like adding new channels to our cable TV viewing list. Once we have access to them, we are able to view them. Just because we don't yet see them doesn't mean they aren't there - it just means we have not subscribed to their existence.

Some people *have* tuned in. According to B. Harris (1993), "A person who can perceive multidimensional aspects of reality is psychic" For clarification, I am not referring to psychics as what some might automatically think of as someone who makes money channeling the dead or telling the future. For the purpose of this discussion, I am only referring to the vast number of individuals who have some degree of psychic connection to multiple dimensions.

Psychics are "normal" people who view realities like everyone else might view a split-screen television. They sense everyday things like everyone else sees, but occasionally, they sense more. What they sense is similar to intuition but it is more intense than intuition. This is really the primary distinction between psychics and non-psychics.

Very normal people with psychic abilities may see backwards in time (déjà vu) or they may see things before they actually happen. In addition, they may see the present with an secondary layer of information. This is best understood when someone is in the present has an overwhelming sense that something else is happening around them. They may or not understand what it is. Sometimes, this "something else" feels compelling but it is vague and fuzzy; other times it is crystal clear.

Another characteristic of people with psychic tendencies is that their physical and emotional senses be suddenly be interrupted by something that feels like it belongs to another dimension. For example, someone who is psychic may be going on about his business then receive sensory input that does not fit the current reality. One way to explain this is that it is a lot like listening to a radio when suddenly, other "noise" cuts into the frequency. This "noise" from another radio station or radio frequency might be faint or it might be blaring. The disruption might be pleasant or unwelcomed and disturbing.

All of this changes nothing about my personal paranormal experience. It just gives me something interesting to think about when I have difficulty falling asleep. Even though I say this somewhat sarcastically, I do not wish to minimize the fact that I sincerely take comfort in the possibility there is something beyond my current reality and physical existence.

CHAPTER SIX`

INVISIBLE SHACKLES

Invisible shackles of another dimension still hold the haunted lovers of the Castillo De San Marcos. For whatever reason they remain inside the darkness of the massive coquina rock walls where they died of dehydration and starvation. Still, I believe their experience is similar to those of us who are living. I believe shackles we create for ourselves are made from negative emotions such as fear, bitterness, hatred, jealousy, and regret. I also believe that if we fail to take action to remove these shackles, we will spend our life (and potentially eternity) as prisoners.

The thing that perplexes me most about the orbs and misty apparitions is their lingering presence. Their shackles no longer bind them so they are free to go where they wish. Don't they know they are free? Is something holding them in that location? Are they there by choice?

It is unlikely I will never know the answers to these questions.

So, in response to the plea of a spirit voice I have told this tragic story. As a reader, you are an equal component in this equation, because *you* are "them" in the whispered phrase, "T-e-l-l t-h-e-m." Quite possibly, together as author and reader, we hold the key that unshackles these spirits held captive for over three hundred years. Undoubtedly, they have long since paid for whatever unjust or immoral sins they were alleged to have committed. It is my sincere hope that the haunted lovers of Castillo de San Marcos are finally released into eternal peace where they can enjoy the presence of a merciful and loving God.

CHAPTER SEVEN

WORDS OF CAUTION

General Warning

Seeking an experience with the paranormal may result in an unpredictable, unexpected, or undesirable consequence; caution is advised.

Physical and Emotional Harm

There are documented stories of individuals who have been physically and emotionally harmed as the result of contact with paranormal entities. The reason for this seems to be that one can never truly predict if the encounter will be "friendly" or "dark" and possibly demonic in nature. As a result, there should always be a conscious awareness that an encounter could result in negative emotions (i.e., depression and suicidal or homicidal thoughts) as well as physical signs and/or symptoms.

Opening the Door

People intentionally or unintentionally provide an opening for paranormal activity to occur. This is usually done through the use of Ouija boards, dowsing rods, and/or séances.

Another way people intentionally or unintentionally provide an opening for paranormal activity is through their disrespecting of sacred ground. Native American land, battlegrounds, burial grounds, and other similar locations are places where paranormal activity may manifest if disrespected.

Finally, there seems to be a steady rise in the amount of hobbyists who "search" for ghosts and other paranormal activity. These ghost hunters, toting an assortment of sophisticated electronic devices and cameras, often go to locations where paranormal activity has been reported. There, they often provoke spirits by speaking to them directly and asking them to do something to make their presence known.

As for myself, I would never intentionally do anything to provoke something paranormal. I would not do this for three reasons: (1) I was taught to be very respectful of all things paranormal; (2) I do not want a paranormal entity to attach its negative energy to me then "follow" me home, because it could have a negative impact on my family as well as myself, and; (3) I do not want to set myself up for interaction with a demonic entity.

CHAPTER EIGHT

MORE INFORMATION

The Holy Bible contains useful information on demons, angels, other unseen spirits, and God. The Biblical information can be a bit difficult to comprehend. Consequently, it should be studied in the full context as opposed to merely extracting specific verses.

In addition, there are a number of interesting television series that offer attempt to further our understanding of the paranormal. While they may be a somewhat sensationalized perspective, they do attempt to present a candid view of paranormal activity with a scientific "twist". A few of my favorites include:

The Dead Files (www.travelchannel.com/tv-shows/the-dead-files)

Paranormal State (www.aetv.com/paranormal-state) and the group around which the television program - **Paranormal Research Society** (www.paranormalresearchsociety.org)

Ghost Adventures (www.travelchannel.com/tv-shows/ghost-adventures) The Ghost Adventures crew produced an episode at Castillo de San Marcos (Season 2 Episode 2).

While there are many ominous tales of demonic activity and pain inflicted upon individuals, one of the most disturbing can be found in the book by Lester Sumrall, "Bitten by Devils: The Supernatural Account of a Young Girl Bitten by Unseen Demons" (ISBN: 0937580988).

REFERENCES

Bloomfield, M. (1883). *Bloomfield's historical guide,*
embracing an account of the antiquities of St.
Augustine, Florida. St. Augustine, Florida: Library of
Congress.

Harrington, J. C., Manucy, A. C., & Goggin, J. M. (1956).
Archeological excavations in the courtyard of Castillo
de San Marcos, St. Augustine, Florida (Bulletin Number
One ed.). St. Augustine, Florida: St. Augustine
Historical Society.

Whitfield, M.D., C. L. (1993). Appendix: Boundaries,
energy and the body. In B. Harris (Ed.), *Spiritual*
Awakenings (p. 235). Deerfield Beach, FL 33442-8190:
Health Communications, Inc.

ABOUT THE AUTHOR

Mary Jordan is a special education teacher and university adjunct professor. She has specific interest in equal rights advocacy for individuals with disabilities. In addition, she has authored www.careerchangesolutions.com.

www.ingramcontent.com/pod-product-compliance
Lightning Source LLC
LaVergne TN
LVHW072106070426
835509LV00002B/30